My Town Used To Be Small

Marvin Buckley

2

factory

3

The big factory needed workers.
New people moved to my town.

workers

The new people needed somewhere to live.
New houses were built in my town.

5

store

The people needed a place to play.
New parks were built in my town.

park

My town grew and grew.
It's much bigger now.

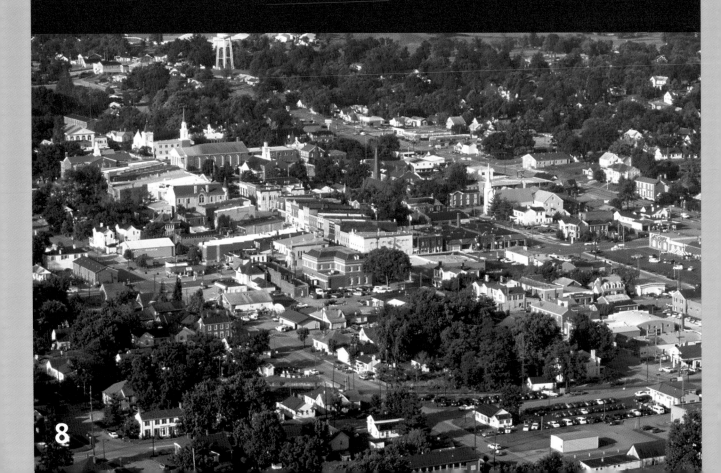